DINOSAURS

CARNIVORES

Have an adult help you remove the stickers.

Phidal

© **2009 Produced and Published by Phidal Publishing, Inc.**
5740 Ferrier, Montreal, Quebec, Canada H4P 1M7
All rights reserved.

UK Address: Highland Farm, Southend Rd.,
Retterdon Common Chelmsford, Essex, UK CM3 8EB

Contact us at **customer@phidal.com**
Visit us at **www.phidal.com**

Text: Azad Injejikian

Printed in Malaysia.

D1224451

Did You Know That?

Carnivorous dinosaurs were meat-eaters that hunted or scavenged for their food. Use your stickers to find out more about these titans of the past.

The name "dinosaur" is made of two Greek words: *deinos* (fearfully great) and *sauros* (lizard).

The jaws of the Tyrannosaurus were big enough to swallow a human whole!

Velociraptors had a sickle-shaped claw on each foot.

The Spinosaurus may have used the big sail on its back to scare off other dinosaurs.

Fossils show that the Nqwebasaurus swallowed rocks to help it digest food.

The Baryonyx is the only dinosaur known to have an appetite for fish.

The tiny Compsognathus
ate insects, small lizards,
and primitive mammals.

The Cryolophosaurus, which means
"cold crested lizard," was
found in Antarctica.

Velociraptors were fast-running
predators with hollow bones
and big brains.

The hollow bones and long legs
of a Gallimimus allowed it to
run as fast as an ostrich.

Troodons, who are thought to be the
smartest of all dinosaurs, were probably
as bright as today's birds.

The large eyes of the Leaellynasaura
helped it see better when it
hunted for food at night.

Carnivore Facts

Carnivorous dinosaurs didn't get along very well. Many of their bones have been found with bite marks made by other carnivores!

The arms of a Tyrannosaurus were so small that they couldn't even bring food to its mouth!

Scientists calculated how fast dinosaurs ran by measuring their bone lengths and fossilized footprints.

Oviraptor fossils have been found next to their nests, which could mean they guarded their babies and eggs at any cost.

The Giganotosaurus was the biggest known land carnivore.

Unlike most dinosaurs, the Sinornithosaurus had feathers instead of leathery skin.

Archaeologists dig up Allosaurus bones more often than any other carnivorous dinosaur.

Velociraptors hunted in packs because most of their prey was much larger than they were.

The Carnotaurus had knobby eyebrow horns and arms even tinier than those of the Tyrannosaurus!

The Carcharodontosaurus was a large, fierce predator that could even hunt giant herbivores.

The Bambiraptor had many bird-like features, like feathers, wing-shaped arms, and even a wishbone!

The Eoraptor was one of the oldest-known dinosaurs. It lived 228 million years ago!

The thin crest on the head of the Dilophosaurus was probably only for display, and not a weapon.

Prehistoric Predators

Carnivores relied on their strength and hunting skills for survival. Bring this scene to life with your stickers.

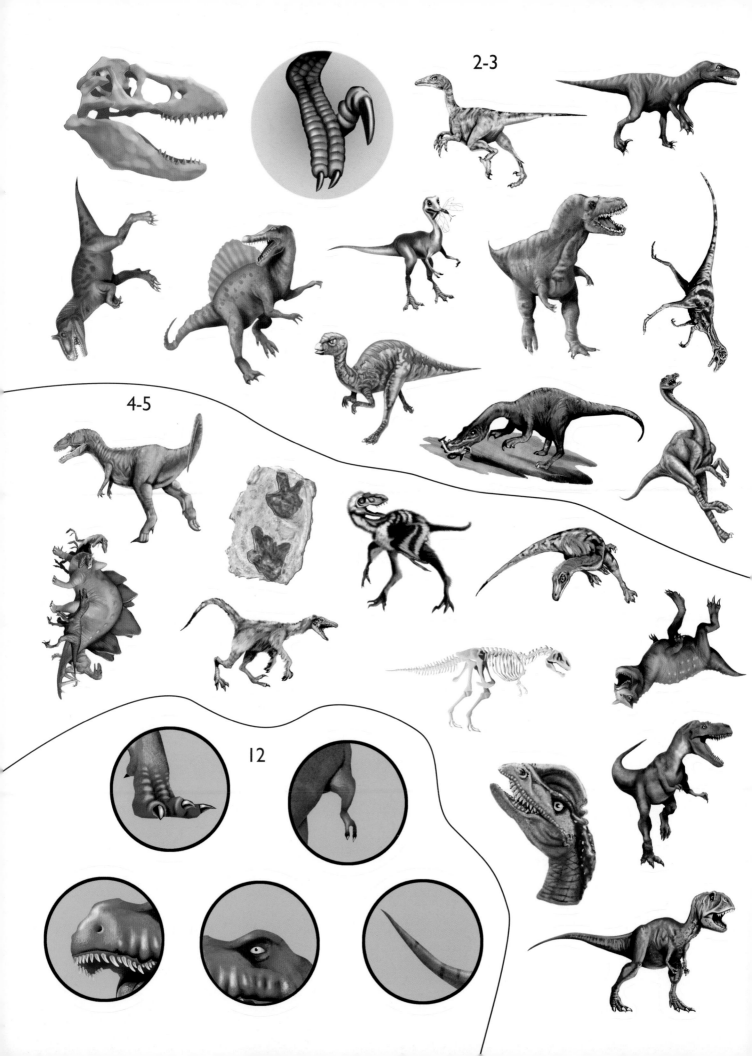

2-3

4-5

12

6-11

13

16

14-15

Close-Up: The T. Rex

The Tyrannosaurus rex was the most powerful carnivore to ever walk the Earth. Discover what made the T. rex the perfect predator.

Its sharp teeth were the length of bananas!

The T. rex's eyes were close together, which helped it spot its prey more easily.

It used its tail to balance the weight of its enormous head.

The small arms of a T. rex were actually three times stronger than ours!

The T. rex ran up to 25 miles per hour.

The Life Cycle of the Tyrannosaurus

Follow the life of the Tyrannosaurus to see how a young carnivore grew up to be a top predator.

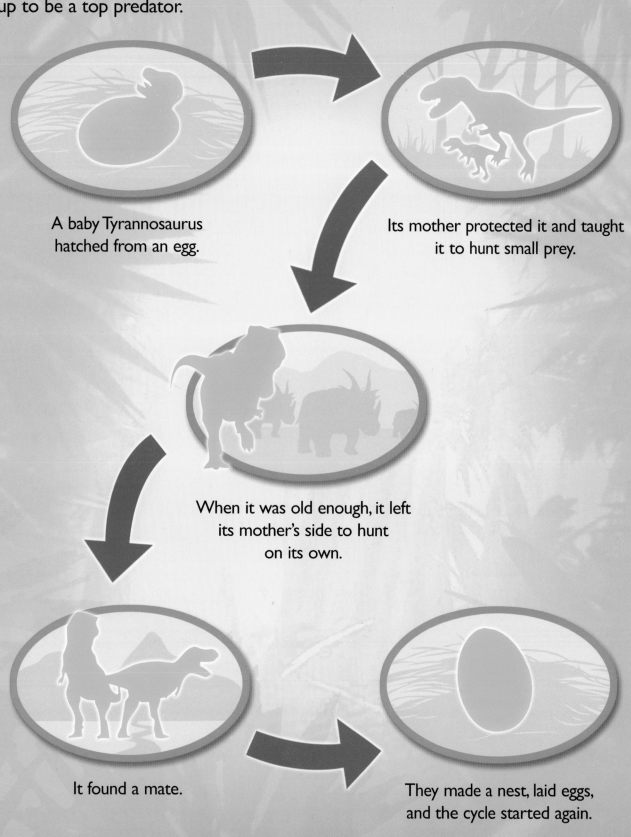

A baby Tyrannosaurus hatched from an egg.

Its mother protected it and taught it to hunt small prey.

When it was old enough, it left its mother's side to hunt on its own.

It found a mate.

They made a nest, laid eggs, and the cycle started again.

Where Were They Found?

Carnivores have been found on every continent in the world, even Antarctica! Match your stickers with their appropriate country.

Baryonyx
England

Allosaurus
USA

Cryolophosaurus
Antarctica

Megaraptor
Argentina

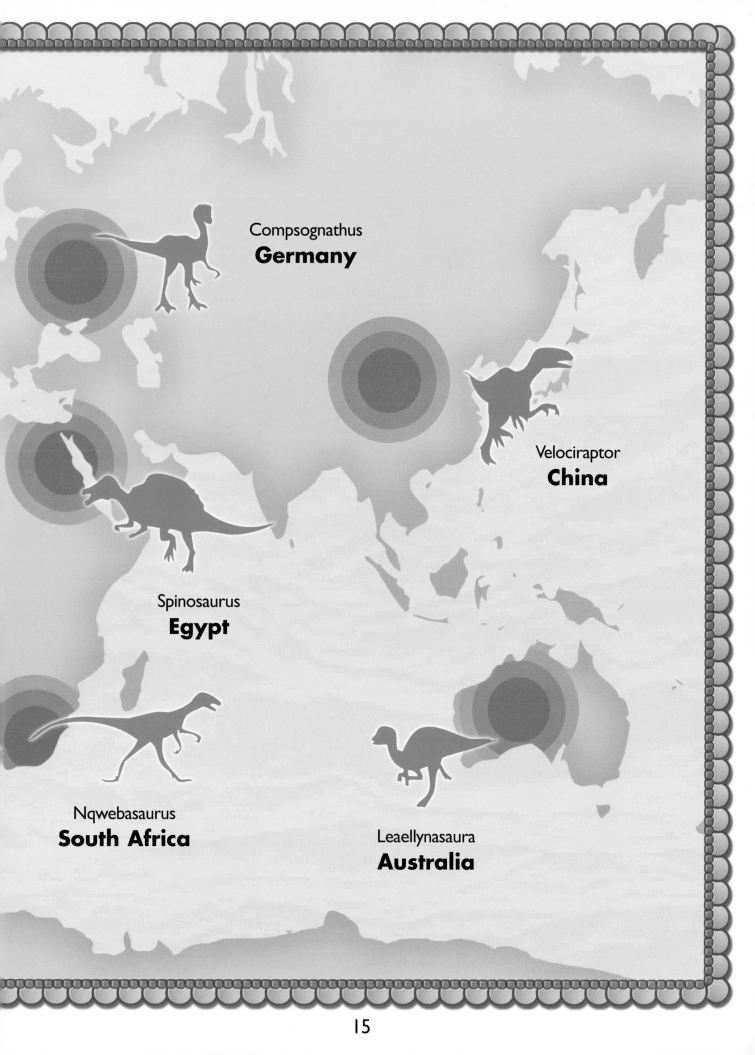

Compsognathus
Germany

Velociraptor
China

Spinosaurus
Egypt

Nqwebasaurus
South Africa

Leaellynasaura
Australia

Can You Spot...

Guess which sticker matches each of these shadows.

Carcharodontosaurus

Gallimimus

Allosaurus

Compsognathus

Bambiraptor